Jake and in the Balloon of Doom

Written by Chris Bradford

Illustrated by Korky Paul

Collins

"Look! Zebra!" said Jake Jones, the explorer.

2

Jen, the hot-air balloon pilot, flew low over the wild zebra. "That newborn is so cute."

3

"The newborn should stay with its mum," said Jake. "There's a lion!"

4

"Let's rescue her," said Jen. She waved her arms to chase the lion away.

5

"SCRAM!" Jen yelled. But her hand hit the balloon's burner.

The flame blazed and the blue balloon flew
high into the air.

"My shirt is stuck!" shrieked Jen.
Jake pulled her away.

The shirt ripped and part of the burner
broke off.

"What now?" Jake asked.

The balloon rocketed up. Jen needed to let some hot air escape.

But she could not reach the rope to leak the air out.

Then the burner fell silent. "No fuel!" said Jen.

They were helpless as the wind blew
the balloon along.

Then they saw a bird.
"It's a kite!" grinned Jake.

He stopped grinning when the rude kite
pecked a hole.

The balloon burst and flew out of control.

Jake and Jen gripped the balloon's capsule.
"We're doomed!" they screeched.

The balloon crashed down, but Jake and
Jen were not hurt.

The crash made the zebra jump in fright ...
and the lion too!

Their cat mewed and struck out at their older sibling, Shane. Shane dropped the pin. He stood on it. "Ow!"

Jake and Jen sniggered. "You popped our balloon, so the lion got its claws into you!"

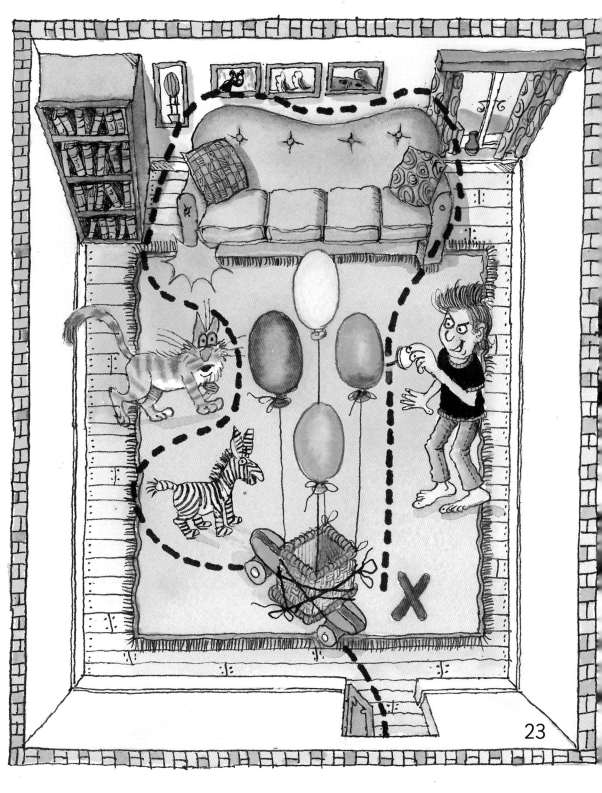

🐾 Review: After reading 🐾

Use your assessment from hearing the children read to choose any GPCs, words or tricky words that need additional practice.

Read 1: Decoding

- Ask the children to read these words and sort them into groups according to how the /oo/ /yoo/ sound is spelt:
  blue, newborn, stood, flew, foot, cute, continue, rude

- Can the children think of one more word to go in each group? (e.g. *ue: true, ew: blew, oo: wood, u-e: tune*)

Read 2: Prosody

- Choose two double page spreads and model reading with expression to the children. Ask the children to have a go at reading the same pages with expression.
- Show children how you use different voices for the narrator, Jake and Jen and how you look out for exclamation marks to add emphasis.
- Reread the whole book to model fluency and rhythm in the story.

Read 3: Comprehension

- Turn to pages 22 and 23 and talk together about how the events in Jen and Jake's story are linked to things in their living room.
- For every question ask the children how they know the answer. Ask:
  - On pages 6 and 7, what made the burner blaze and the balloon go higher? (*Jen waving and hitting the burner*)
  - On page 11, which word shows that Jen had a problem? (*couldn't – which means "could not"*)
  - On page 17, what two things did Jake and Jen do which show they were scared? (*gripped the balloon's capsule, screamed that they were doomed*)
  - What is the name of Jake and Jen's older brother? (*Shane*)
  - On pages 20 and 21, what clues are there that show Jen and Jake's adventure was imaginary? (e.g. *a toy zebra, the pin popping the balloon, the cat instead of a lion*)